TEMPLE SAGRADA FAMÍLIA

Text: Jordi Bonet i Armengol

Photographs, design, lay-out and printing, entirely created by the technical department of EDITORIAL ESCUDO DE ORO, S.A.

3rd Edition

I.S.B.N. 84-378-1470-7

Dep. Legal B. 39350-1999

Editorial Escudo de Oro, S.A.

PRESENTATION

When looking at the immense city of Barcelona from a distance, one quickly picks out the tall and daring pinnacles that rise to the heavens in search of infinity. They are the eight belltowers of the two façades of the temple of the Sagrada Familia, a church that is more than architecture It is poetry. And like all true poetry, it is a portent of eternity. That is why this temple has never been finished. Gothic cathedrals were never finished either. Today, the simple clear eyes of visitors ecstatically admire the symphonic harmony of stones in play and song, in praise of the Lord.

The temple of the Sagrada Familia is a true cathedral. It is known as the ''the new cathedral of Barcelona'': of the twenty-first century. The anonymous faith of the poor and humble erects this temple in its magnanimity, amidst the great capital like an oasis of peace. It is there to show future generations the presence of the Christian faith, living and functioning at the very roots of the Catalan people.

Today everyone in Barcelona loves it, this rhythm of the Sagrada Familia. And all other Catalans, as well. It was conceived one day by an architectural genius, Antoni Gaudí, ''the great builder of this century,'' in words of Le Corbusier. He was a man who put his soul into everything he did. And his soul was profoundly Christian. And what this genius did best was conceive of religious symbols and Catholic temples. This one, the Sagrada Familia, is truly ''the ecstasy of a mystic.''

The belltowers of the Sagrada Familia, with their tall pinnacles, have become the most expressive symbol of the city of Barcelona. Who would have said as much! The rest have been left behind, small and limited. The temple rises like a majestic tree, with the gradualness of that which dominates space and time. It slowly grows, broadening the horizons of human life, so that the men and women of our country will not have to live oppressed by the vulgarity of cold and gross materialism. The temple pinnacles, like an advance on eternity, point to the blue of heaven, reminding one of the vocation every human person has of one day meeting with God in the fullness of life with no end.

Meanwhile, the splendidly worked stones of our grand sanctuary speak to us today of a new world and of a new earth. This is the new world and new earth of brotherly love, of generous understanding, of living together in peace, of a solid and firm faith fed by the grace of God. Amidst the ideological pluralism we live in our society today, men and women from Barcelona and elsewhere without exception have, in the temple of the Sagrada Familia, a reference point of unquestionable hope. ''It is an open cathedral,'' said the poet Maragall. ''It seems as if it wants to embrace the entire city; and those who approach the open arms of its walls will feel the warmth of its embrace.''

There are those who are surprised to see a Catholic cathedral being built in our time. Why? ''The temple of the Sagrada Familia is built by the people,'' said Gaudí. And he added that it was a work in the hands of God and the will of the citizens. And so it is.

The reader of these pages written with such care and love by the architect Jordi Bonet i Armengol, can follow the immense wealth of the work of Gaudí, who said that great temples have never been the work of a single architect. He began the construction and left the plans of this temple. Today, his disciples faithfully follow the lessons of the Master. One can perfectly say, then, that the spirit of Gaudí lives in the work of the temple of the Sagrada Familia: the greatest sanctuary created today in Catalonia.

Cardinal Narcís Jubany

City of Barcelona, with its port and factories, at the foot of Montjuic.

1. THE HISTORICAL SETTING

The Sagrada Familia is the product of the circumstances stemming from its founding and the unique drive of Antoni Gaudí who dedicated more than forty years of his life as an architect to it.

During the last years of the nineteenth century and the first of the twentieth, the people of Catalonia strongly demonstrated the determination to reaffirm their cultural roots and, as a national entity, make a contribution to humanity.

Catalonia was a small country that after flourishing for centuries and achieving a certain leadership among the many people Western Europe, lost much of its importance in the great ferment of world events at the beginning of the Modern Era.

Romanticism, together with the crisis of Spain in the nineteenth century, stirred nationalist feeling in the Catalan people, in turn, leading to the recovery of their language, until then relegated to the family circle. It acquired new vigour determined to attain the institutions which had exercised secular rule over it. The Catholic faith, a strong presence at the origins of Catalonia in the tenth century, again played a leading role in the nation's rebirth — ''La Renaixença'' — a thousand years later.

By the side of factories and the silent labour of workers, multitudes of saints and founders emerged

Santa Maria de Montserrat.

anxious to do good. A country priest and poet, Jacint Verdaguer, was a major force in restoring the dignity of the Catalan language, while a prospering Barcelona furnished a powerful capital where, thanks to the growth of commerce and the economy, a flowering of artists could now express themselves. Catalonia could once again communicate its unique personality to the world beyond its borders.

At a difficult moment for the Universal Church, a Barcelona bookseller, Josep M. Bocabella, organised the Association of Followers of St. Joseph, which with half a million members economically assisted the Holy Father, setting itself the goal of building a temple dedicated to the Holy Family.

In 1881, the year of the celebration of the millenium of Montserrat, Leon XIII proclaimed Our Lady of

Founder, Josep M. Bocabella.

Montserrat patron saint of Catalonia, and on December 31st of the same year, the Association purchased the largest parcel of land in Barcelona's Eixample district. The corner-stone of the new temple was laid on the following 19th of March, St. Joseph's day.

Had this structure been the project of the diocesan architect F. de Villar, originally commissioned for the job, the temple would, in all probability, have been quietly lost in the history of architecture. However, when the walls of the crypt were barely a metre high, differences between founders and architect surfaced and a promising new architect, Antoni Gaudí i Cornet, was assigned to take over the project. The date was November 3, 1883.

I.2. FOUNDING AND CORNER-STONE

a) *The Association of Followers of St. Joseph.*
On October 1, 1866 approval of this Association was
decreed, authorising its founder Josep M. Bocabella
— bookseller — to publish a bulletin which began in
December, entitled "The Propagator of the Devotion
of St. Joseph". Its first objective was defense of the
Church. With half a million members in 1878, including the Holy Father and the King, its objective
was to spiritually and materially help the Holy See
and raise a monumental expiatory temple, surrounded
by gardens, dedicated to the Holy Family, and where
proper public leisure activities would accompany
learning and spiritual contemplation.

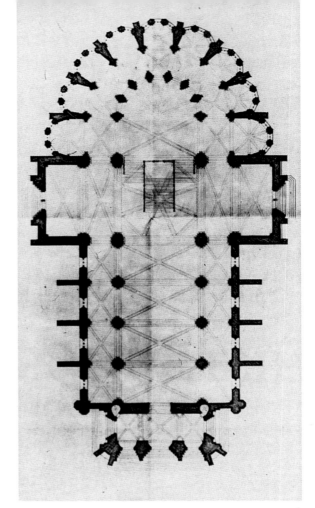

Layout of project by architect Villar.

Outline and west façade.

b) *The corner-stone. March 19, 1882.*

The notary document bears witness that the bishop of Barcelona, Josep M. Urquinaona i Bidot, cloaked in the sacred ornaments and attended by the bishop-elect of Vic, Josep Morgades, and other clergy, in the presence of the Captain General and other authorities, of Josep M. Bocabella and Manuel de Dalmases representing the Association of Followers of St. Joseph, of the architect F.P. de Villar, Elias Rogent, director of the School of Architecture, and a panoply of faithful, solemnly proceeded to the blessing of the terrain, placing the foundation-stone of a Monumental Expiatory Temple, to the greater glory of the Holy Family, to ''awaken indifferent hearts from their slumber. Exalt the faith. Promote Charity. Invoke the Lord to have mercy on this Country, and encouraged by its Catholic roots, to think, preach and practice virtue'' (text of the parchment placed in the corner-stone).

Rendering of laying of the corner-stone ceremony.

Aurora Altisent

Antoni Gaudí i Cornet.

I.3. GAUDI, ARCHITECT OF THE TEMPLE

Antoni Gaudí, born June 26, 1852, was baptised at the church of St. Peter, of Reus, then the second city of Catalonia. The future architect's family were coppersmiths who struggled to give the young Gaudí an education. Reus was a vigourous and prosperous provincial town that would, in a few years, produce other men of great renown: Joan Prim, the general who became president of the Spanish government, and Marià Fortuny, the painter who was famous in Europe at the middle of the nineteenth century. Having obtained his architectural degree from the School of Architecture of Barcelona in 1878, Gaudí soon distinguished himself in his field and received commissions from the man who would be his friend and patron, Eusebi Güell i Bacigalupi, as well as from the prestigious architect, Joan Martorell, who introduced him to the temple of the Sagrada Familia. Along with his vocation as an architect, the activity of Antoni Gaudí extended to several fields. As a hiker and nature enthusiast he became member of the Centre Excursionista de Catalunya and visited and studied monuments and countries: Roussillon, Mallorca, Montserrat, Toulouse, the peaks of the Pyrenees, etc. As a music lover, including the opera and choral music, he was connected with the Orfeó Català; and with workers' and cooperative movements, through the Cooperativa Mataronense. He actively participated in many acts and groups promoting Catalanian patriotism, where he entered into contact with Father Jacint Verdaguer, Angel Guimerà, Narcis Oller, Marià Aguiló, J. Masriera, J. Collell, etc. As a member of the Artistic Circle of Saint Luke, from its founding until his death, and of the Spiritual League of Our Lady of Montserrat, he had a strong friendship with the man who would later be bishop of Vic, Dr. Torras i Bages. He was also a friend of Joan Maragall, who was the great propagator of the Sagrada Familia. The most universal and permanent values that made Gaudí a world figure are the fruit of his faith, expressed in purposeful research and the study of historical forms and the thought behind his architectural vision, much like a priest of architecture. This faith gave him a delight in knowledge and in the need for Love as the highest conception of beauty: that is, of GOD CREATOR.

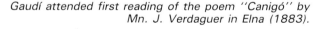

Gaudí attended first reading of the poem ''Canigó'' by Mn. J. Verdaguer in Elna (1883).

An idea of the whole temple. Original drawing by Gaudí.

II. A GENERAL DESCRIPTION

Antoni Gaudí envisaged the temple of the Sagrada Familia emerging from the urban landscape of Barcelona in dramatic verticality. The temple has a basilical floor-plan, with five naves and three transepts. The interior is 90 m long and the transept 60 m wide; the central nave measures 15 m. The apse is bordered by 7 chapels and 2 circular stairways, with an ambulatory around the presbytery. An exterior cloister circles the building and connects the three main entrance façades: to the east, the Nativity; to the west, the Passion, and to the south, the Glory. Each façade is crowned by four belltowers about 100 m high symbolising the twelve apostles. There are sacristies at each corner of the apse wall. The chapel of the Holy Sacrament and the Baptistry occupy the corners at both sides of the Glory façade. A dome 170 m high rises in the centre of the transept representing Jesus Christ, flanked by another four symbolising the evangelists, and covering the apse a final dome dedicated to Our Lady.

The four belltowers crowning the Nativity and Passion façades, emerge from the outline of the city's buildings.

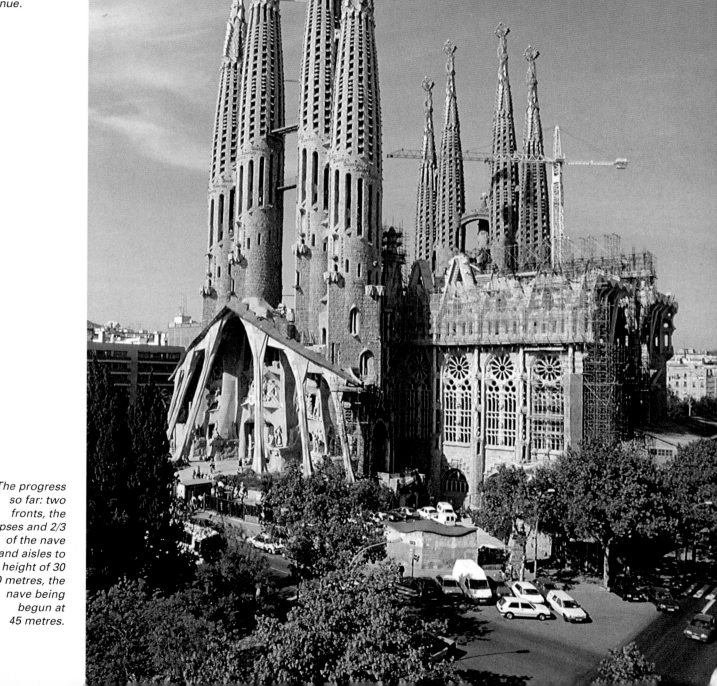

The temple in the evening, as seen from Gaudí Avenue.

The progress so far: two fronts, the apses and 2/3 of the nave and aisles to a height of 30 30 metres, the nave being begun at 45 metres.

Interior wall of the east façade.

II. 1. THE FLOOR-PLAN

The structure is shaped like a Latin cross, although the longest arm is almost as long, from the transept to the back of the apse, as the Portal of Glory. Gaudí maintained the placement of the axis with which his predecessor had begun the temple, although he would rather have placed it diagonally. It consists of three naves, the lateral ones 7.5 m and the central one 15 m wide, with two more that occupy the choir at the back of the transept; all together, the main nave is 45 m wide. A large area 30 x 30 m, that is, a 900 sq m surface area with four central columns, occupies the centre of the transept, rising to a height of 60 m. This area is encircled by the cloister and the three portals, with two sacristies on each side of the apse and the chapels of the Baptism and of the Penitence on both sides of the façade of Glory. The portals extend out, with two large very differentiated porches allowing the placement of all the iconography of the Nativity, of the Passion and of the life of the militant and triumphant Church, the Glory.

Each column is dedicated to an apostle or to the Catalan bishoprics, of Spain and of the five continents, with the saints that made them flower, in a synthesis of the universality of the Church extending from east to west, similar to the order the first bishop of Tarragona, St. Fructuos, prayed for at the moment of his martyrdom.

Current state of the construction: nave and columns.

General layout of the ''Templo Expiatorio de la Sagrada Familia,'' with its symbolism and dedication.

Key of the vault of the crypt: the Annunciation (A).

Engraving representing the work on the crypt (B).

Lengthwise view of the crypt (C).

II. 2. THE CRYPT

Gaudí maintained the already commenced floor-plan of the crypt, but raised the vault which covered it, with a beautiful representation of the Annunciation of Mary, at the key, so that the window would illuminate the spot above the ambulatory which surrounded it and separated it from the chapels. He also introduced a wide moat surrounding the crypt to keep out humidity and admit light.

The chapels are dedicated to the members of the Holy Family of Jesus. In the centre, the Sacred Heart, flanked by the Immaculate Conception and St. Joseph, along with St. Joachim, St. Anne, St. Elizabeth, and St. Zacharias, St. John the Baptist and St. John the Evangelist. In 1885 the altar of St. Joseph was inaugurated, with neo-Gothic ornamentation that Gaudí had studied in detail.

Portal of the Sacristy (Aa). Altar of Our Lady of Montserrat (B). View of the ambulatory (C). Layout of crypt (D). (page 17).

(A)

(C)   *(B)*

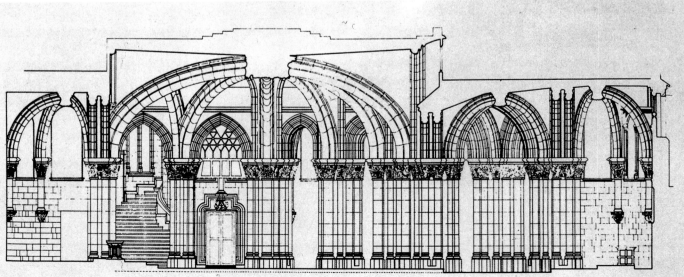

(A)

(B)

(C)

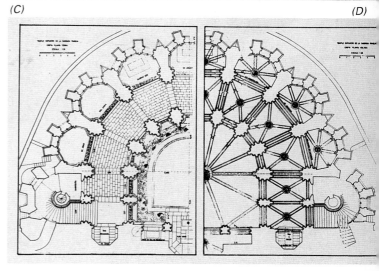
(D)

At this time, the crypt is where parish life takes place. The main altar occupies the central area of the transept. The Holy Sacrament is on one side and the image of Our Lady of Montserrat is worshipped on the other. The graves of the Bocabella and Dalmases family and of the architect Antoni Gaudí are in the chapels around the ambulatory. A mosaic representing the vine and grain follows the perimeter.

Back of the crypt (page 18).

Detail of capitals and vaults (A).

Chapel of Carmen. Tomb of Antoni Gaudí (B).

Chapel of St. Joseph (1885) (C).

II. 3. THE APSE

The apse, built between 1891 and 1895, is of neo-Gothic architecture, although there are elements where the personality of Gaudí stands out. It consists of seven polygonal-shaped chapels dedicated

Snails in the needles.

Needles of the apse. Vertically composed chapels and windows.

Pinnacles with clipped vegetal shapes.

Clipped against the sky, humble tassel.

to the suffering and joy of St. Joseph. At the crown we have the antiphonies of Advent, beginning with O; the placement of the windows; the contrast of light and shadow in the chapels, and, especially, the gargoyles and needles of the pinnacles inspired in the flora and fauna which grew around the temple. Lizards, snails — land and sea —, frogs and toads, salamanders, etc., and enlarged shoots of vegetation constitute an extraordinary naturalist view in the service of architecture.

The pedestal and the baldachin of the Founding Saints, Dominic, Anthony, Benedict, Elias, Bruno, Francis, Clare, Bernard and Teresa, are placed along the support walls of the chapels.

Sprouts of flora surrounding the temple, enlarged in Montjuic stone.

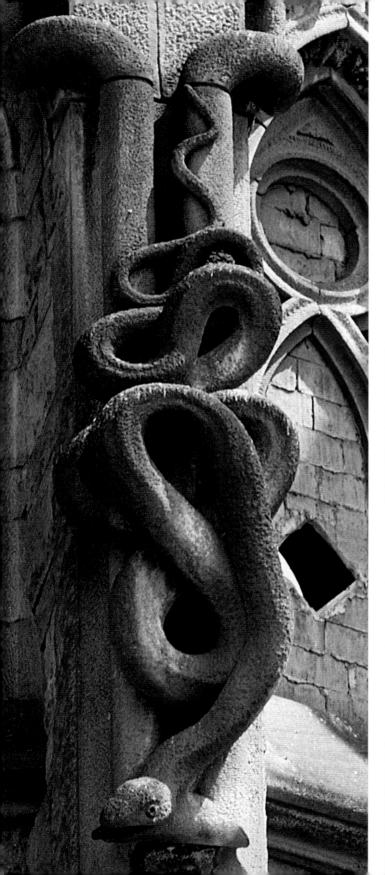

A watersnake curled around a drainage pipe.

The colour of the Nativity needles contrasts with the sprouts and natural elements of the apse.

Decorative effects in contrast: nature and geometry.

The walls of the apse solitarily rose over the plain of Barcelona at the end of the XIX century.

Ther verticality of the counterforts and naturalistic decoration.

Symphonies of stone and colour (pages 24/25).

Gargoyles, with reptiles from the surroundings.

View of the skylight of the Roser. Beginning of the cloister.

II. 4. THE CLOISTER

The layout of the cloister encircling the temple differs a great deal from that of other basilicas, monasteries, or cathedrals.

This feature connects the portals, chapels and sacristies and, by encircling the temple, allows processions to circulate, while keeping out noise. Located on the ground floor of the temple, there is space below which can be used for workshops, services or storerooms.

Initially, Gaudí constructed the two first sections on each side of the Nativity façade, placing portals dedicated to Our Lady, in advocations of the Roser and Montserrat, in the irregular space connecting the belltowers. These portals cover conically enveloping lanterns through which light enters.

Interior. Brackets, columns, play of lights.

*The Portal
of Roser.
(1899).*

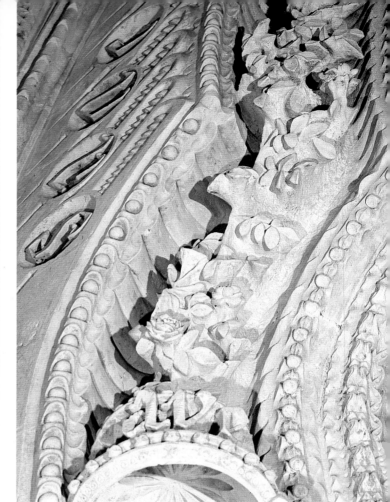

The temptation of woman: vanity.

The temptation of man: violence.

Each section is covered by a groined vault from which pediments traversed by large windows in the façade separated by small columns with helicoidal-shaped bases and capitals emerge

Gaudí finished the section corresponding to Our Lady of the Roser with extraordinarily fine touches. It is filigree work, reminding one of needlepoint or basket work, surrounded by roses and rosaries. Our Lady of the Roser, with the Infant, presides the archivolt of the portal with St. Dominic and St. Catherine of Sienna. At each side of the portal are the Patriarchs, Kings and Prophets, Isaac, Jacob, David and Solomon.

On the corbels of the groins of the vaults are the representations of the Death the Just and the temptations of Man and Woman. The text of the ''Ave Maria'' invites expression of the angelical salutation, and the words ''Et in hora mortis nostrae. Amen,'' give meaning to to the company of Jesus, Mary and Joseph, comforting the dying.

The temptations show the devil placing a bomb in the hand of a terrorist and a purse in that of a woman prostitute.

The key of the vault is an extraordinary composition of three angelical figures dancing. The sculptural work was closely supervised by Gaudí himself.

The revolutionary madness of 1936 burned the doors and destroyed an important part of the figures made of fragile stone of Vilafranca. This group, lighting the conical lantern crowning the upper part of this most inspired example of turn-of-the-century Gaudí, has been carefully cleaned and restored.

Decorative detail, recalling basketwork (A). Roses surround the archivolt of the portal (B). The Death of the Just (C). Cloister capital (D). (page 28).

Detail of Our Lady of the Roser, St. Dominic and St. Catherine, illuminated by light from the skylight, between roses and rosaries.

Key of the vault of the first section of the cloister. Three angelical figures dance and play in the foam.

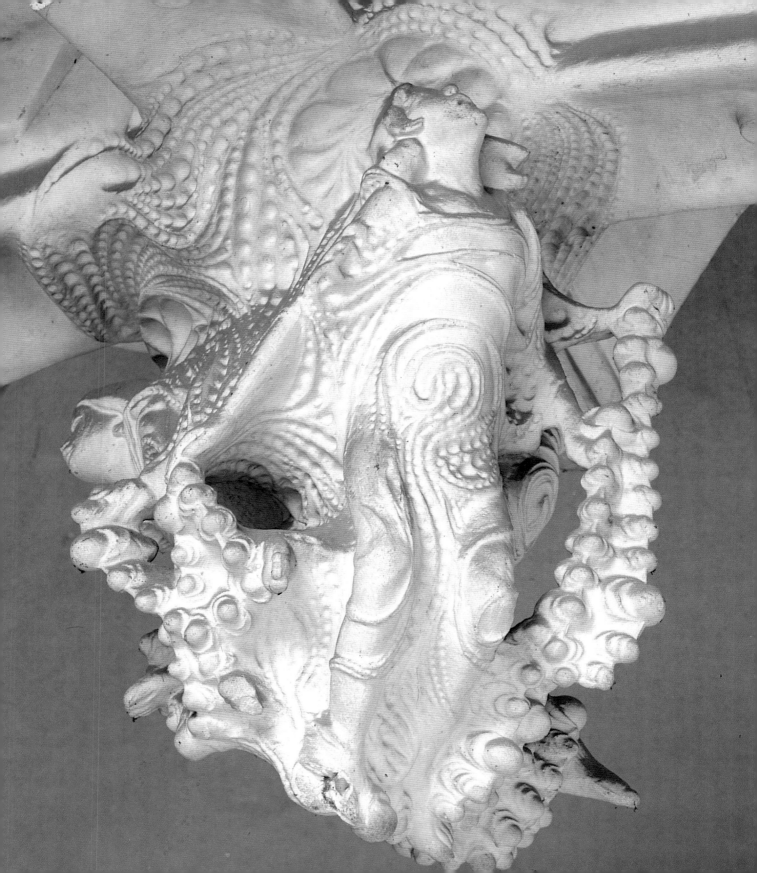

II. 5. THE NAVES

The naves consist of totally new forms with original geometrical and stuctural solutions.

They are the result of years of reflection and planning. Gaudí began the study of these naves in about 1910. He incorporated his experiences with the chapel of the Güell Colony. A solution with slightly helicoidal columns, arches and vaults, using hyperbolic paraboloids, was published in 1917.

The discovery of the luminosity of hyperboloids led to their use in the nave in a concave-convex intersection of domes coordinated with columns, walls and windows, and materialized in 1/10 scale models. This

Set of models of façades and vaults of the naves and roofs of the temple, just as they were exhibited at the time of Gaudí.

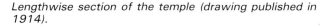

Lengthwise section of the temple (drawing published in 1914).

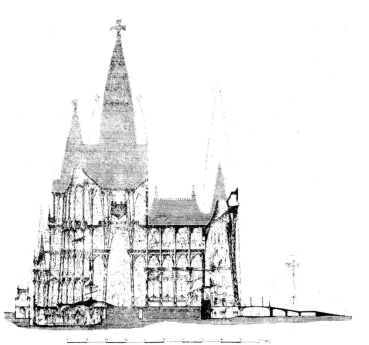

unit constitutes a vision of the forest which often served him as an image to explain his project.

Gaudí considered these columns, vaults, high windows and roofs to be the final version, and a general and structural presentation of them was made by his assistant, the architect Sugrañes, before the Catalan Architect's Association in 1923. Gaudí's 1/10 scale model is now being converted into a full-scale reality.

Upper part of the vaults of the central nave (1/10 scale).

a) *The columns.*

This new form of vertical support conceived by Gaudí, leaning slightly "so as to follow the pressure curve supporting the weight of the roof," constitutes an extraordinary creative solution.

It is the result of years of fully documented research and demonstrates the untiring dedication of Gaudí in search of a totally new and surprisingly beautiful element.

Geometrically, it consists of the twists of helicoids in turn begetting starred polygons rounded off by parabolic curves, where they would be the indentations of 6, 8, 10 and 12-pointed stars, depending on their placement, diameter and the weight each one must support.

These columns follow a simple generation wherein the diameter, height, construction sections and, above all, constant and different relationships are all inter-connected. This is the result of the intersection of two helicoids turning in opposite directions. The first turn begins at the base of the column, to the same height in metres as the polygon has sides.

Flutes issue from the intersection beginning at the concave parts of the starred polygon and multiplying upward as they turn. The second reaches a height in metres of half the sides of the polygon and produces twice the number of new flutes. A final turn of the fourth part of the height quadruples them up to the beginning of the corresponding capital. Thus if the original polygon is 6, 8, 10 or 12-pointed, the

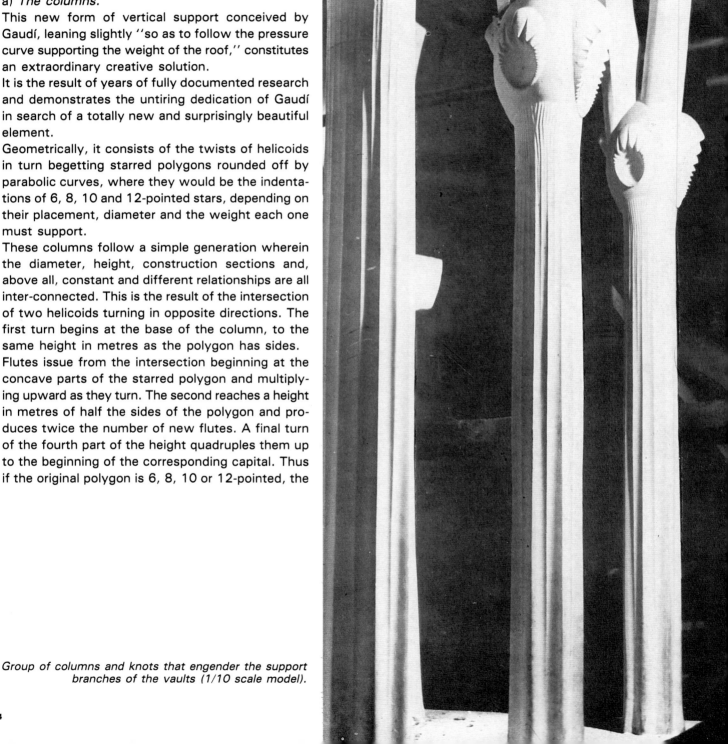

Group of columns and knots that engender the support branches of the vaults (1/10 scale model).

Knot or capital, convergence of the ellipsoids. Original model (1/10 scale) restored.

Plan of the columns issuing from starred polygons rounded off by paraboloids, of 6, 8, 10 and 12 points.

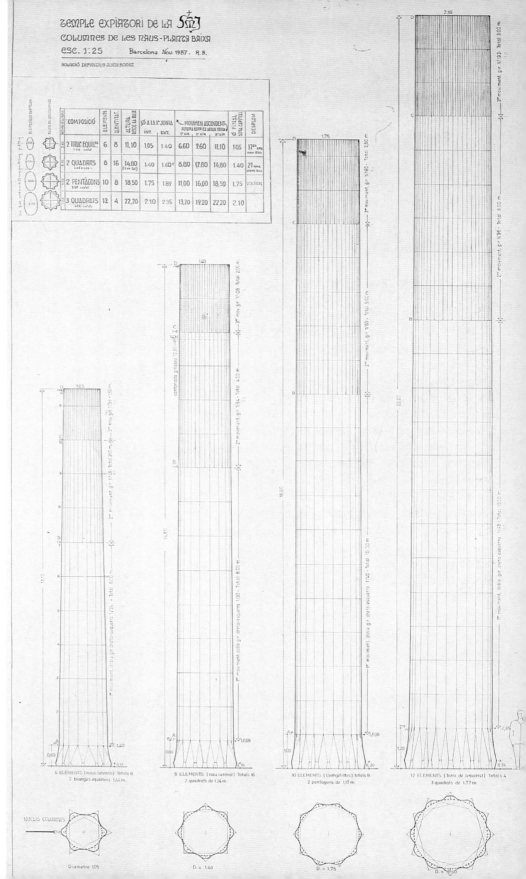

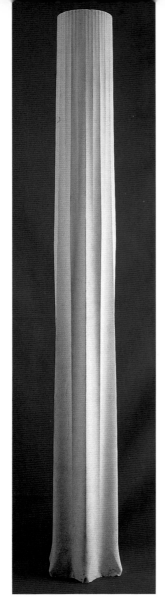

1/10 scale model of a six-sided column.

number of flutes will be 12, 16, 20 or 24, to be followed next by 24, 32, 40 and 48, and finally 48, 64, 80 and 96.

Gaudí's column is at once extraordinary and simple; it begets flutes which become finer and multiply as they rise, emerging from the most sunken parts of each flute. As it ascends, at the same time it has both the lightness of helicoidal growth and the gravity of a Doric column, but above all, it is surprising, completely new and exceptionally beautiful.

The Lleida column rises at the east transept.

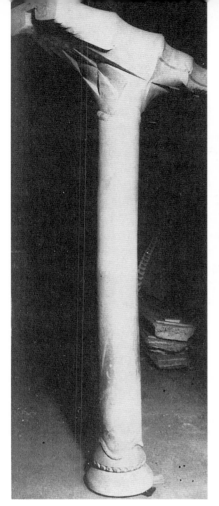
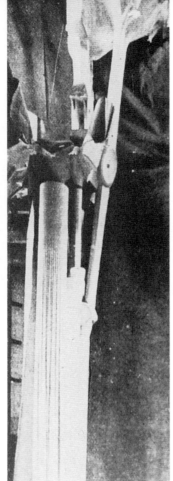
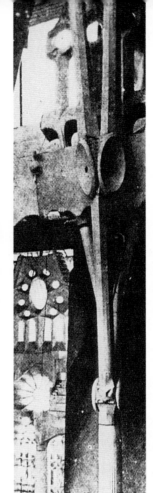
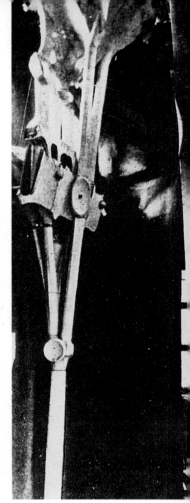

Plaster model of column (1/10 scale) with which Gaudí studied and developed until he reached a final solution.

The columns fork out following the pressure lines to support the vaults. (Photograph of Gaudí's workshop with 1/10 scale models).

Photograph of Gaudí's workshop with experimental solutions of the columns.

b) *The vaults.*

Atop the columns, the capitals are large oval-shaped elements that gather in the upper part of the column; from them, similarly generated new columns rise like branches, leaning in so as to reduce the span of the vaults. The latter are made up of several ruled surfaces: revolving, direct or inverted hyperboloids, a profusion of other geometrical forms resulting from their intersection, with circular orifices or slits, for light and ventilation, forming part of the starred, pyramidally open or closed enclosing surfaces of the section.

The intersection of these surfaces forms the tense and lightened ensemble that, as seen in the 1/10 scale model, is by itself one of the achievements — though only in plaster — which best establishes the contribution of Gaudí to the architecture of this century.

The vaults are rich in symbols and figures with anagrams of Jesus, Mary and Joseph on the centre lanterns, and mosaics with angelical figures surrounding the figure of the Heavenly Father, at the back of the apse, the central piece of the ornamental mysticism Gaudí dreamt of.

Original model by Gaudí of intersections of direct and inverted hyperboloids that form the vaults.

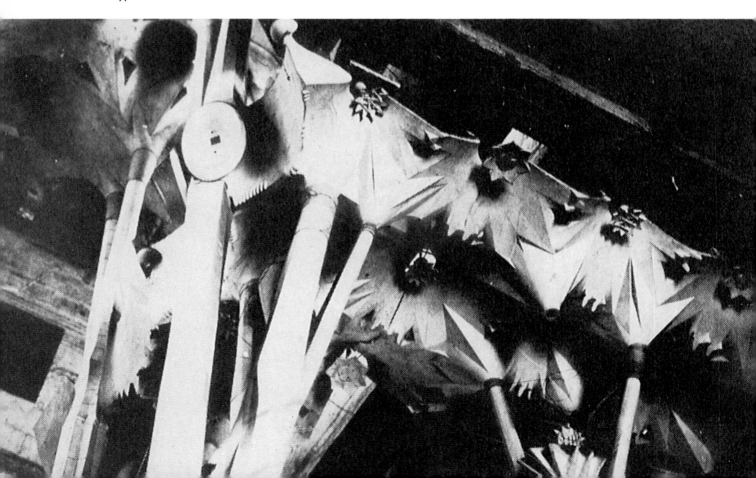

*Plaster
model of
the vaults
(1/10
scale).*

Columns and side vaults and long windows built in 1996.

Detail of the 1/10 scale model of the lateral and central vaults.

The intersections of the hyperboloids generate starred forms, while light penetrates through the ports of these hyperboloids like light through the foliage of a forest.

Original model (1/10 scale) of a window of the upper lateral nave.

c) *The windows.*

Along the large nave and the transept, slim windows enclose the temple allowing light to filter in through geometrical forms that begin at the neo-Gothic sides on the Nativity façade, to next change into inscribed appliqués of paraboloids, revolving and flat paraboloids, hyperboloids that, as Gaudí expressed, makes mouldings unnecessary, since light enters and is diffused in a play of varying intensity and colour.

The first «orange» spire, now completed, in the transept.

Detail of a window of the lateral nave beneath the choir.

Original model of the terminal pinnacle of a window (1/10 scale); group of paraboloids that gather the fruits of the harvest like a basket.

Gaudí studied four solutions before arriving at one he considered final:
1. Neo-Gothic.
2. Paraboloids following neo-Gothic envelopment.
3. Paraboloids and hyperboloids.
4. Paraboloids and hyperboloids, but with an ellipse with four apertures.

On the outside, they are decorated with the fruits of each season, following their seasonal cycle. They symbolize the rain of the fruits of the Holy Spirit which all men receive. On the mullion at the top of each window a Founding Saint is placed: Ignatius of Loyola, Josep de Calasanz, Dominic de Guzman, Ramon de Peñafort, Francis de Paul, Teresa de Jesus,

Original model (1/10 scale) of the window of the central nave.

Joachima de Vedruna, Antoni Maria Claret and John Bosco. There are windows on the lateral naves that rise to a height of 30 m, and at a second level lighting the central nave, to between 30 and 45 m. The lower section follows Gothic design, i.e., pointed arches, but at the highest ones there are rose windows formed by hyperboloids, with all the richness of Gaudian geometry. Topping these windows are baskets brimming with all kinds of fruits.

Drawing of the same window resulting from the starred intersections of the hyperboloids.

Interior of the
long windows
in the nave.

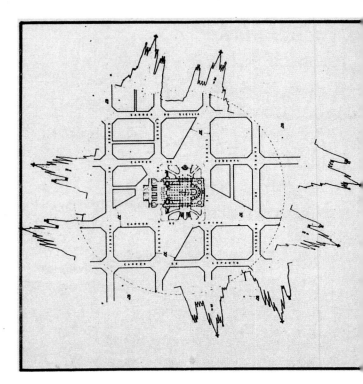

The silhouette of the temple as Gaudí drew it from different perspectives.

d) *The roofs*

They constitute one of the unique elements of the temple, and with their verticality they will be one of the most outstanding features despite their functionalism — protection against rain and the elements —.

''A monumental unit of six domes lights the transept, the altar, and constitutes the exaltation of the temple,'' aid Gaudí, ''culminating in a pyramidal outline of the building.'' In the last years of continuous work on the building, Gaudí had readied the structural study of the building, but there were only sketches that showed a structure similar to that of the sacristies, though longer, and with an eight-pointed star cross section rounded off by concave paraboloids. Twelve and thirteen stories divide the great height with small columns and a sturdy double shell, with unfaced brick and stone on the outside. The dome of Our Lady covers the apse, which because of its breadth, appears as a cupola.

The roof of the skylight of the cloister shows the solution reached with stone slabs.

Original model of the roof of the nave.

Restored 1/25 scale model of the naves and roofs of the temple and façades of the Nativity and of the Passion.

Weather-resistant stone from Montjuic has been proposed for the outer layer of the roof. With its structural supports — floors and small columns, and the vaults that make up its interior view —, Gaudí's principle is always present: "Divide the inert loads and multiply the active elements".

Restored original model (1/10 scale) of the skylight of the lateral naves.

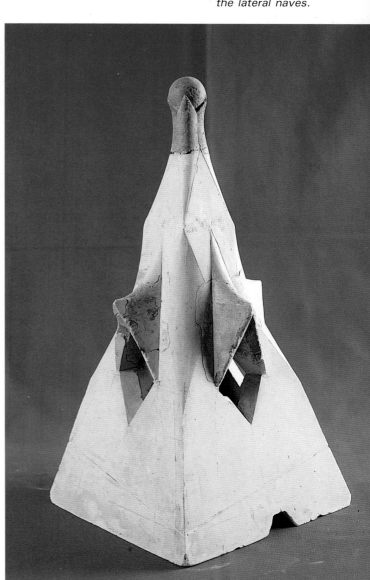

The roof of the central nave is formed by pyramids — one per section — interconnected and with large paraboloids in the front of the windows.

Small structures bearing the anagrams of the Sagrada Familia support and crown lanterns 70 m high, with the words, ALLELUIA. AMEN, on parabolic shields.

The space between the vaults and the roof is horizontally divided into four floors which support groups of four small inclined columns that rise above the higher ramifications of the main columns.

The lateral naves are covered by slightly sloping surfaces, and feature beautifully resolved, pyramidal-shaped lanterns that light the rafters and, because they are in front of the windows, split the light.

Drawing of the temple following the indications of the Master, as done by Lluis Bonet i Garí.

6. THE FAÇADES

The life of Jesus is represented on the east and west façades: Nativity, Passion and Resurrection.
The main façade — the Glory — portrays the divine power of judgement of Jesus Christ, and man in front of the transcendental order of his Creation. All have three portals symbolizing the theological virtues of Faith, Hope and Charity. Each of the subjects rises to its highest point. The four belltowers also ascend representing the Apostles. On it SANCTUS, SANCTUS, SANCTUS, HOSANA EXCELSIS can be repeatedly read. Gaudí's idea for all viewers of the Temple to praise the Lord by reading the inscriptions.

Present night-time view of the temple.

Drawing published in 1906, entitled "The Dream Come True."

The four belltowers of the belltower of the Nativity façade.

Present view of Nativity façade from Plaza Gaudí.

Nativity Façade.

It is the great work, done and nearly finished by Gaudí himself. Its intent is to express the joy of all creation with the birth of Jesus, the son of God incarnate, born of the Virgin Mary.

A very important bequest made the erecting of this façade possible; the foundations were begun in 1894. Gaudí explained: "It is not possible for one generation to erect the entire temple; let us then leave such a forceful example of our passing, that the coming generations will feel the urge to do as much or more." In 1906, the newspaper "La Veu de Catalunya" published a drawing of the temple viewed from the Nativity façade, entitled "The Dream Come True."

At the central archivolt, there are stars, animals and mid-winter plants, beneath the Star of the Bethlehem, Jesus, Mary and Joseph, between the ox and the mule, surrounded by musician and singing angels. These three figures of the Holy Family are situated above a column helicoidally encircled by the names of the genealogy of Jesus, since Abraham, Isaac and Jacob. A wrought iron grille protects it. On both sides, are the Adoration of the Shepherds and the Magi. Further up, angels play bronze trumpets announcing the joyous event of Christmas. The Annunciation and the coronation of Mary are superposed; finally, a large cypress tree, a refuge for birds, symbolises the Church, like an immense pinnacle topped by a Tau, the Greek letter for the name of God.

The three portals of the Nativity façade and the Four Apostles nominally represented by each belltower.

J. Busquet's sculpture of the Holy Family, under the star of the Kings and the archivolt with the signs of the zodiac and the birds celebrating the Nativity.

Angels with bronze horns announcing the birth of the Saviour.

Portal of Hope. The Flight to Egypt and the Killing of the Innocents. Joseph with the Child.

Portal of Faith. The Visitation. Jesus among the doctors, is found by Joseph and Mary. Jesus the Worker.

Paeans with tame fowl.

Decorative floral elements.

The Killing of the Innocents.

The pinnacle of the portal of Hope, a crag of Montserrat.

The pinnacle of the portal of Faith. The Immaculate Conception and wheat tassels.

Detail of the Jesus the Worker.

Detail of icicles, palm fronds and the horn-playing angels.

On the south side, there is Hope, the espousal of Mary and Joseph, the flight to Egypt, the massacre of the Innocents, the ship of the Church steered by St. Joseph, and at the pinnacle a crag of Montserrat, with the inscription ''Salveu-nos'' (Save Us). On the other side, we have Faith. We have represented the Visitation, Jesus among the doctors and the presentation at the Temple, and Jesus the labourer at his carpenter's bench. On the pinnacles, we see ears of wheat and grapes, and the image of Mary in the dogma of the Immaculate Conception.

The façade as a whole is the triumph of life; facing east, it receives the rising sun, and represents the joy of light that, with the Word made flesh, lives in us. As in the ''Cant dels ocells'' (The Song of the Birds), the popular Catalan song, here there are 36 birds in adoration of the infant Jesus.

*Detail of
the pinnacle
of Faith.*

Original drawing by Gaudí, from the Passion façade.

Façade of the Passion.
To the west, distress, nakedness, pain, sacrifice, death contrast with the Nativity façade, and should preside at the death of the Just One, above all to announce the Resurrection and Ascension to Heaven, of Jesus Christ.

Gaudí repeated that, had he started with this façade, people would have reproached him; compared with the Nativity, which is ornamental, ornate, turgid, Death is hard, bare, seemingly made of bones.

The façade was projected in grief when Gaudí was ill in Puigcerdà. With time to study and meditate on this portal, he said: "I am ready to sacrifice the building itself, smash arches, chop down columns, if only to give an idea of how terrible the sacrifice is." Through an archway supported by six large inclined columns, like ornaments or large, rooted, sequoia-like trunks, an immense pediment rises with eighteen smaller bone-like columns supporting a smaller archway. The later life of Jesus is represented. The lack

The sculptor Josep M. Subirachs works on the sculptures relating the Passion and Death of Jesus Christ.

Bases of the columns of the Passion portico, a composition of paraboloids. Comparison with sequoia trunk.

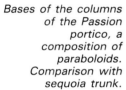

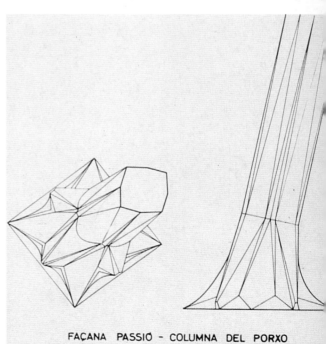

FAÇANA PASSIÓ - COLUMNA DEL PORXO

Jesus of the column.

of ornamentation concentrates the tragedy in the main dramatic events presided over by the figure of a naked Christ at the supreme moment of Death. The sculptor Josep M. Subirachs is making one hundred sculptures evoking the Passion. He has begun with the figure of Christ on the column, on the mullion of the central portal. Standing alone, there is the figure of Christ bound. On both sides, the betrayal of Judas and the denial of Peter, the disciples He said would betray and deny him. Higher up, the Via Dolorosa: Jesus is bearing the Cross after being condemned before Pilate. The legendary figure of Veronica centres the scene, showing the negative image of the ''man of sorrow,'' the image of a face we barely see, surrounded in mystery, in the portrayal of the Last Supper, where we see Jesus from the back surrounded by the disciples receiving his Body and Blood, and in the fallen, invisible, disfigured head at the gloomy instant of death. Mary, St. John, the Holy Women, soldiers, the people, etc. Slowly, these sculptures will be installed, ending with the Sepulchre. The image of the Resurrected Christ, at the level of the large window of the transept, in the Ascension between the belltowers, will end the portrayal of the life of Christ, facing west, in the catechistical interpretation of the Mystery of our salvation.

Detail.

The Passion façade. Present state.

The Passion portico. Inclined columns, composed of paraboloids.

Veronica shows the image of Christ suffering among soldiers and witnesses.

Fragment. «Ecce Homo».

Detail, Mary, with Jesus in her lap.

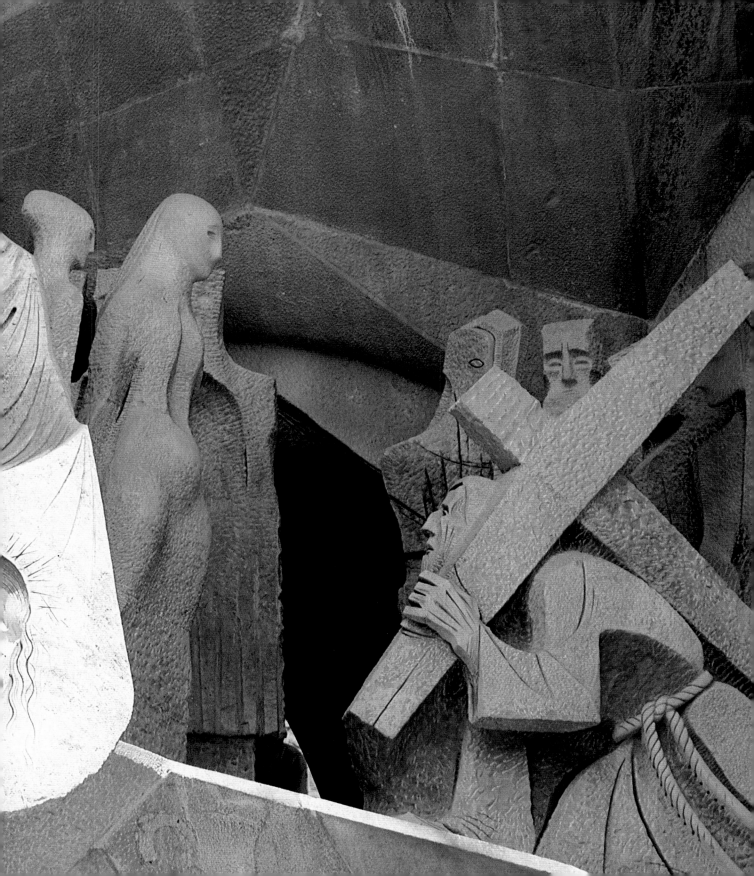

The Via Dolorosa. (pages 72/73).

Glory Façade.

Gaudí left a study of the volumes and structure and the iconographic and symbolic design of this main façade facing towards the sea.

A monumental narthex gives way to the three portals and is crowned by four belltowers flanked by the chapel of the Sacrament and the Baptistry. Altogether there are 11 doors leading directly to the chapel or through the cloister, and from them to the interior of the temple. The central portal consists of three doors. The narthex is covered by the vaults beneath the belltower, hyperboloids, and 15 lanterns. These are asymmetrical hyperboloids which section cones. They visibly rest on 21 columns except the connecting walls between chapels and beneath the belltowers. This all forms a grand tympanum with the ascending hyperboloids, where Gaudí imagined the iconographic representation of the Glory.

Clouds of stone bear written on them the symbol of faith — the Credo—. The entrance, at the same level as the temple, is high enough above Mallorca Street for this route to continue circulating below and in this manner the narthex opens onto a great platform and stairway extending out onto a large open space. On each side, Gaudí imagined a waterspout twenty metres high and an enormous flaming cresset — purifying water and fire —. Iconographically, he presents Man in the order of creation, his origin and his end, and the way to achieve it. From Adam and Eve, through labour and the practice of virtue, man can obtain the Glory that through redemption Jesus Christ has opened for us, with the help of Grace. We also find the Beatitudes, the virtues and the capital sins; hell is represented beneath the vaults of the street, and higher up, purgatory. There is a petition from the Our Father above each of the seven entrance doors to the temple, representing the Sacraments. In the very centre of the façade, we see St. Joseph working, bearing the badges of the manual arts and trades. Higher up, Mary presides queen-like over the saints, and at the top is Jesus Christ, with the attributes of the Passion, with the seven angels with horns summoning to the Last Judgement. All of the angelical hierarchies surround the Eternal Father; and, in the large central rose window, the Holy Spirit completes the trinitary picture.

Original fragments of the study of the Glory façade (currently being restored).

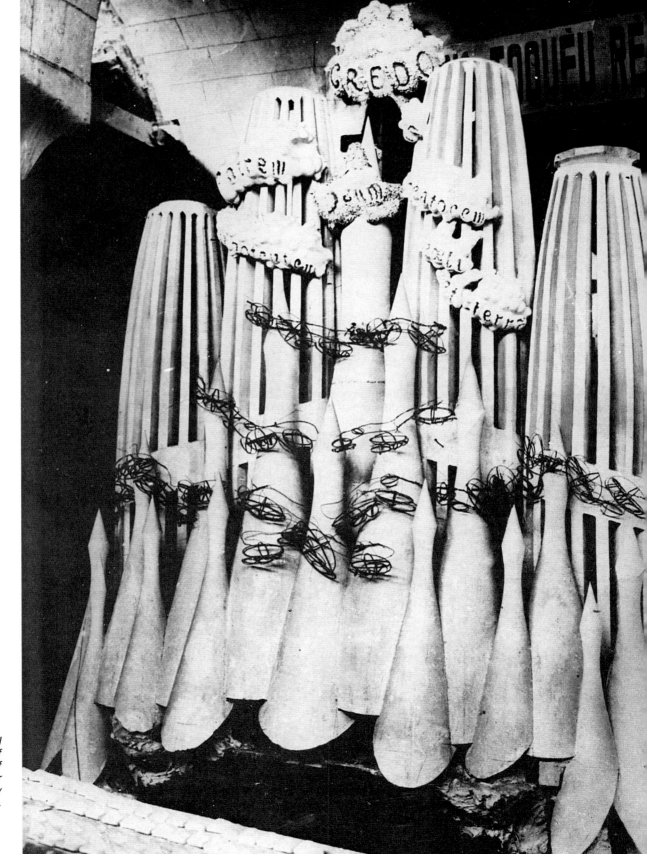

*Original
model of
the study of
masses for
the Glory
façade.*

II.7. SINGULAR CHAPELS AND SACRISTIES

''The paraboloid is the father of all geometry,'' Gaudí would say; and with an extraordinary composition of these planes he projected the double-faced cupola-like structures situated in the north and west corners of the cloister, atop 13 × 18 m rectangles 46.5 m high. These elegantly shift from 8 sides to the 12 higher sides by making the vertexes of 12 unequal pediments agree. The floor is the section of the 12 spherical lunes of slightly unequal hyperbolic paraboloids. Their are several floors for community services, and the cloister encircles them leaving the corners covered by lanterns dedicated to the Ember days of autumn and to Advent. The cupola arris and the large parabolic spherical lunes of the extrados, of visible brick, are very light and will be decorated with mosaics.

At the centre of the main axis of the temple, in the middle of the NW wing of the cloister, Gaudí projected the chapel of the Assumption. There are drawings explaining the composition of the little chapel, a reminder of the popular adornments that celebrate Our Lady of August and were possibly suggested by the work of the sculptor Bonifaç in the cathedral of Girona.

The Baptistry and the chapel of the Sacrament occupy the corners of the main façade. A rough sketch by Gaudí shows a structure supported with central columns with the penetration and enveloping of the cloister.

Externally similar to the sacristies, they also have small chapels and lanterns dedicated to the Ember days of Lent and Pentecost in the corners.

Original drawing by Gaudí. Sacristy.

First study for the Passion façade.

Gaudí original for chapel of the Assumption.

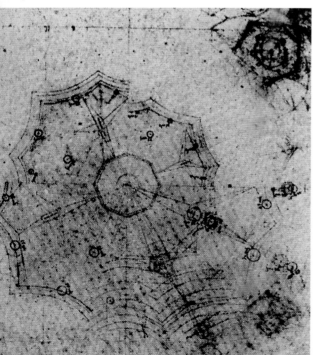

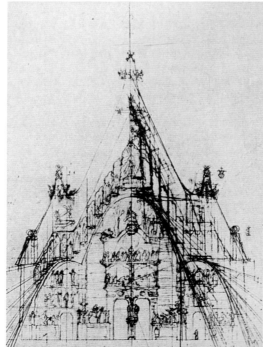

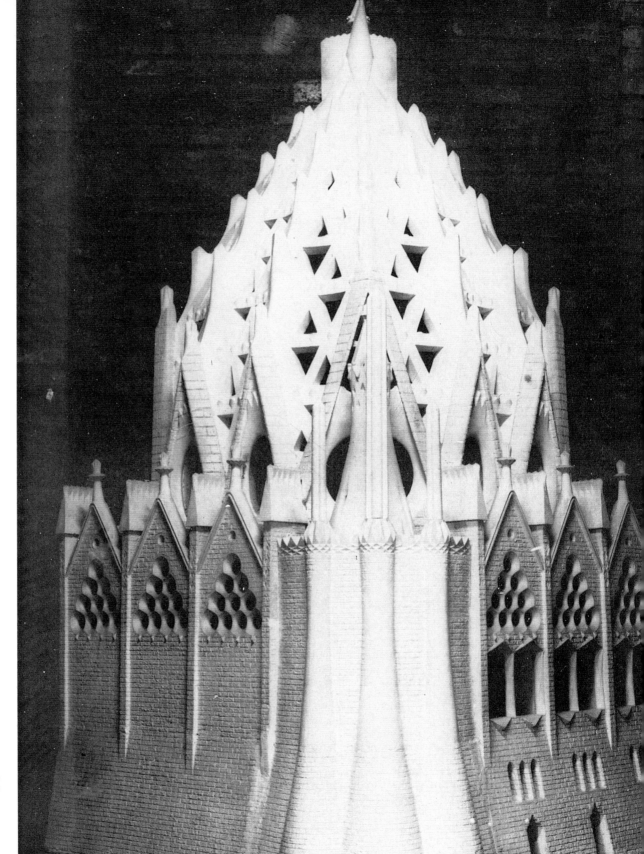

Plaster model of the sacristy.

II. THE BELLTOWERS AND DOMES

On November 30, 1925 the first belltower to St. Barnabas was revealed. Gaudí mentioned his pleasure at seeing "how that peak brought together heaven and earth." The other three were finished by the architect Sugrañes, Gaudí's successor and collaborator, who left the Nativity façade almost finished. There are 12 belltowers projected. They will symbolise the 12 Apostles and rise 98 to 112 m above the floor of the temple. Eight are now finished corresponding to:

The Nativity façade: St. Mathew, St. Jude, St. Simon and St. Barnabas.

The Passion façade: St. James, St. Bartholomew, St. Thomas and St. Phillip.

Still missing are those of the Glory façade, dedicated to: St. Andrew, St. Peter, St. Paul and St. James.

The temple as seen from the east. Study done under the direction of Puig Boada and Bonet Garí.

A team of
"castellers" raising a
"quatre de vuit."

The four east
belltowers.

Inside a belltower.

Plaster model of the solution (1910) presented in Paris with ''pine-conebeacons,'' modified by Gaudí in the twenties.

Detail of the figure of the Apostle Barnabas of the first belltower Gaudí saw completed.

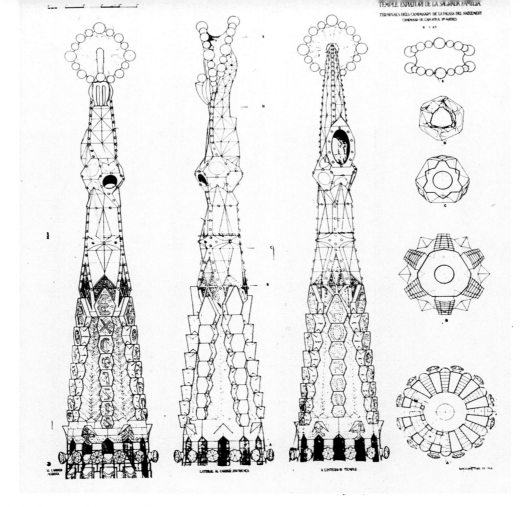

Drawing of the body and layouts of a belltower termination.

The transept and the apse are crowned with another six domes dedicated to Jesus Christ, the Four Evangelists and Our Lady. The tallest will culminate in the Cross 170 m high. In day-time it will sparkle with mosaics, and at night with spotlights it will project on other belltowers and from them onto the city, symbolising the words of Jesus: "I am the light" (John 8, 12). Gaudí worked a long time on the terminations of the belltowers. In the model presented at the Paris Exhibit in 1910, the solution he projected was quite different: so-called "beacon pine cones" received and projected the symbolic light. The lack of resources allowed Gaudí, having more time, to compose geometrical figures symbolising the Apostles with the episcopal attributes: the Ring, the Mitre, the Crosier and the Cross.

The nearly 25 m height of the terminations begin with the letters announcing HOSANNA EXCELSIS, in hexagonally circling ascending order, separating channels formed by dihedral angles decorated with pyramidally encircling dark-green glazed baked brick. Next, starred geometrical forms of gold and silver Venetian mosaics on a red background rise and converge at the confluence of an octahedron and a perforated sphere, which houses the reflectors and represents an Episcopal ring. A triangular pyramidal trunk curves round tracing the Crosier, while two diverging curvilinear squares reveal the Mitre as they trace the Cross, on which the gold radiance of its mosaic shines against the red background and white of the spheres which decorate and terminate the ensemble, the tips of the Cross, like giant flowers, rounding off the point.

The belltowers emerge from the mass of the three

A new architecture. Stone and mosaic. Never-before-projected forms stand out against the blue sky.

large portals of each façade dedicated to the theological virtues: Faith, Hope and Charity.

Beginning at the square bases that these portals house in their intersections, they round off leaving the space that the figures the Apostles occupy atop a pedestal and a pinnacle-shaped baldachin.

The transition to a circular or elliptical ground plan at the Passion façade is thus made, followed by tall ascending windows, interrupted by a section where the words of the SANCTUS invite praise.

Next, sound-wings distributed in hollows that diminish as they rise emerge between the 12 ribs and extend to the highest point, to better distribute the sound of the tubular bells, which were projected to send out musical sounds to the city.

Detail. Mosaic. Baked bricks and basalt cobblestones.

Detail of the starred element with Venetian mosaic.

The telescopic form of the Catalan Gothic belltowers of Santa Maria del Mar or cathedral needles is surpassed by the continuity of the parabolic profile which in ascending produces newly created, unmistakably unique architectural characteristics familar all over the world.

The burst of brilliant gold or silver colour against a blue sky lit by the sun makes the beauty of this unique creation vibrate. Equally admirable on overcast days, it constitutes in its entirety a hymn of praise to God-Creator, just as Gaudí desired the reading the angelical hymn HOSANNA EXCELSIS to be for both believers and non-believers.

Structurally, the belltowers have a double passage, by means of which the helicoidal stairway ascends the interior, threading its way up between the shadows of the ribs of vertical stone and the vertically climbing sound-wings. The interior space foresees the installation of tubular bells which Gaudí studied so the sound would reverberate.

*The
episcopal
symbols!
the cross,
the ring, the
mitre and
the crosier.
Hossana
Excelsis.*

Details of
the
terminations
of the
belltowers.

''Shattering-
'' of
Venetian
mosaics,
gold and
silver, red
and white.

Sculpture.
Polychrome.

Gaudí has
create a new
architecture...

...outlined
against the
blue sky.

II. 9. THE SCHOOLS

For the provisional implementation of the programme of the temple, the parish school was built in 1909-1910, and the partly sunken floor of the lateral naves and a section of the cloisters was set aside for schools. Gaudí would say: ''by the side of the Church, the people will receive education and culture.'' And so he undertook the provisional construction of a suitable low-cost building in a part of the grounds.

Sketch by Le Corbusier on his visit to Barcelona.

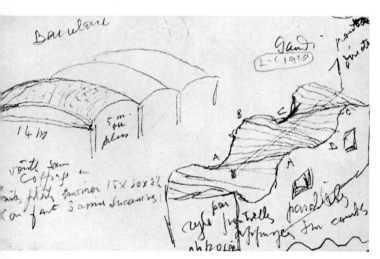

The destroyed schools, July, 1936.

Roof of the schools.

Gaudí demonstrated his great building capacity with a simplicity and complexity that are surprising. Interior inclined vertical partition-walls support beams that hold up an undulated roof, going from concave to convex to collect water, at the same time that it is structurally more resistant. The roofed-over span of the three classrooms was divided in half so that standard-length planks could be employed. That is why standing wooden beams and a crossbeam along the length of the building divide the rectangle around the perimiter.

The fire caused by revolutionary extremists in July 1936 destroyed the schools, which the architect Quintana reconstructed with modifications.

Period photograph of a class.

III. 1. THE STRUCTURE

Gaudí made a first project of the temple based on Gothic type. However, he corrected part of what he thought were its defects. He stressed the verticality of the elements early on, as shown by the sketch of the whole structure, seen from the apse ("The Propagator," 1891).

Trying to eliminate the flying buttresses — "crutches," he called them — by banking the arches, the initial path towards the parabola already found in buildings he was building (Güell Palace 1885-90, Teresian School 1889-92), are accumulated experiences, experiments that, once pondered, would later be used in his temple.

The intelligent and extraordinary decision of raising the Nativity façade, stemming from a very important donation, prolonged the in-depth study of the complete project of the temple. On the contrary, the economic precariousness of the work was a help in that it contributed to the fact that in the last 12 years of Gaudí's life he threw himself into clearing the way that would make the temple the most important structural contribution in the history of architecture of the twentieth century. The unfinished project of the Güell Colony chapel, but with the crypt and mechanical project terminated, was the testing ground for the new theory with which to resolve the mechanical and creative problems and the new architecture offered by his close observation of nature and power of synthesis. With the study of pressure curves, determined that they should coincide with the architectural forms, he decided to lean the columns, identifying the mechanical and architectural organism in each element.

"This tree, next to my workshop, is my master," said Gaudí. That is why he branched out columns above a certain height to divide the dead weight of the vaults by multiplying the active resistant elements. The result was an arboreal, balanced and light-weight structure that would have made it possible, had it been built 70 years ago, to considerably reduce the scaffolding necessary for any Gothic cathedral.

First neo-Gothic project (1890) by Gaudí for the Temple of the Sagrada Familia.

Furthermore, Gaudí chose the most resistant natural materials capable of holding up the heavy loads the other projected domes and roofs of stone supported, at the same time fire-proofing the building, while their loads also helped absorb seismic jolts.

With his assistants, architects Sugrañes and Quintana, the loads, pressure curves and results were studied ("Anuari As. Arq. de Cat. 1923" — Conf. F. Q. 1952), at the same time that by employing secondary grade surfaces, hyperboloids, helicoids and paraboloids, columns were connected with vaults.

The agreement of the column with the central concave hyperboloid matches the convex hyperboloid of the vault, in a contrast of stars, hollows and solids which plays with light in an extraordinary, never-imagined composition. The lightness of the surrounding walls, that in fact are windows without buttresses, transforms the structure of the choir along the sides of the naves into an active structure. The elimination of dead weight lightens the foundation and significantly reduces the volumes and loads and,

Transversal cross-section of the nave with the balanced structure which follows the pressure curves.

Lengthwise section. Study done under the direction of Puig Boada and Bonet Garí.

therefore has an effect on the economy of the work and on execution time.

Gaudí studied these new unprecedented solutions on 1/10 scale models; he left some sections in plaster, unfortunately destroyed in the revolutionary events of July, 1936.

A long and difficult task of restoration of the fragments saved, of casts and originals, with the help of already published plans, has been the great contribution of 25 years of efforts by the disciples of Gaudí: Puig Boada, Bergós, Quintana and Bonet i Garí, with the help of many other persons — architects, modellers, students —. (These models may be seen in the temple museum.) This has allowed new models to be made, plans redrawn and work done on the calculation of the structure. Today, the viability of Gaudí's project has been demonstrated with computers. Architects and co-directors, J. Margarit and C. Buxadé, have assured the work and enthusiastically declare: ''Imagination, structural rigour and the intuitive flash of the tensional plexus of Gaudí, reach their highest point in the project of the Sagrada Familia, and more specifically in the roof of the nave. The skylights and hyperboloids, the paraboloids, pillars and capitals, the light, are the transcription of nature as seen by Gaudí, illuminated by his mysticism in harmony with the spirit of the work, a petrified forest with the help of his profound

Model of the mechanical study of structure and masses, made to calculate and project the chapel of the Güell Colony.

Comparison of the section of the temple of the Sagrada Familia and the cathedral of Cologne. Observe the considerable difference between the sections of the columns and the counterforts of both.

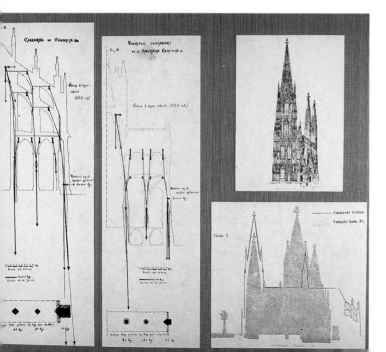

knowledge of geometry, which explains so much of the world around us.''

Shortly before his death, Gaudí, who was extraordinarily demanding in his work, who never improvised, but rather threw himself completely into working out the best solution, declared himself clearly satisfied with the results obtained. He could only object: ''I am sorry I will not be able to see a single section finished'' (of what would be the nave of his temple).

The portal of Charity of the Nativity façade represents a great cypress tree (the Church) where birds (the faithful) may seek shelter.

III. 2. THE SYMBOLISM

"All the temple of the Sagrada Familia is a hymn of praise to God intoned by humanity of which each stone is a verse sung in a clear, powerful and harmonious voice," wrote Puig Boada. It was very clear to Gaudí that it was to be the temple of a people, a song to the Trinity of God. He said: "The shape of the towers — vertical and parabolic — is the bringing together of gravity and light. Reading the Sanctus that helicoidally climbs up them, our gaze will carry us to heaven."

No detail escaped the study and symbolism of the temple he dreamt of: "I have taken forty courses in liturgy," Gaudí answered one day to someone addressing him. Conversations with his friends, the bishops Torras i Bages and Grau i Campins, and his in-depth study of the liturgy let him pick for each element a meaning that would transmit the catechism of the mysteries of the Faith he professed so intensely. It is not strange, then, that on a visit of the Papal nuncio Mns. Rangonessi, Gaudí was told: "You are the Dante of architecture."

On its outside, the temple symbolizes the Church, Jesus Christ and the faithful represented by Mary, the Apostles and the Saints. Seeing it, believers or not, they will praise the Lord God by reading the angelic hymn and admiring the work made by men in honour and glory of the Saviour.

The central dome, dedicated to Jesus Christ, will culminate in the Cross, shining by day with mosaics and at night with rays of light projected on the belltowers and city. It will read: AMEN. ALLELUIA. It will be flanked by the four domes of the Evangelists and one dedicated to Mary, the highest, crowned by an illuminated star. The twelve belltowers represent the Apostles, first bishops of the Church, the voice that exhorts the faithful, witness to the revelation received. Inside, the columns supporting the vaults and the roof also represent the Apostles and the local Churches with their saints, that is, everybody, from the Catalan dioceses to all the continents: heavenly

Termination of the pediment of the cloister. The saw represents Joseph. The shavings form the name of Mary. The cross at the top represents Jesus.

Decorative composition with rosaries.

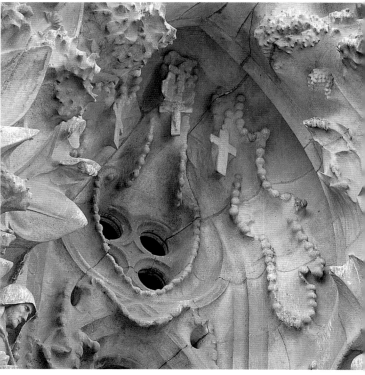

Detail of the candelabrum (wrought iron). The sword that traverses Mary. Alpha and Omega.

"Sursum - Corda,", raise your hearts, can be read at half-way up the belltowers.

Jerusalem, the mystical city of peace the Lamb has won for us.

Gaudí said of the interior naves and vaults of the temple: "It will be like a forest." Light will enter abundantly through windows at various heights. Daily prayers of the Church may be followed in the most important texts, which will be written on the handrails of the choir and the triforiums: the Miserere, the Te Deum, the Benedictus and the Magnificat. In an ecstatic vision, Gaudí explained to visitors just how he imagined the temple, in a twin current of the saints of earth and heaven, and the angels of heaven and earth.

From the columns that encircle the transept and the apse dedicated to the Apostles and the Evangelists, those of the Apostles Peter and Paul stand out, bringing together the triumphal arch with Calvary: the Crucifix, Our Lady and St. John. The representation of the Trinity is thus completed with the Eternal

The Annunciation. The signs of the zodiac are represented on the pointed arch.

Father, which will be seen on the dome of the apse on setting foot in the temple, and a lamp with seven flames representing the Holy Spirit. The written hymn of Glory and the hanging canopy covering the altar, will centre the attention of participants.

On the triforium of the side of the Passion façade, is Our Lady surrounded by angels with the attributes of the litany. At the Nativity, St. Joseph with the tools of his trade will complete, with the Crucifix at the altar, the Holy Family. The representations of the stained glass windows will present the Jesus of the parables: Light, Truth, Life: "I am the resurrection, the water of life, the vine, the Sower, the good Shepherd."

The exterior and interior exhort and make explicit the spiritual life of the Christian, offering all men, all of Humanity, the brotherhood of being a child of God the Father.

III. 3. PLASTICITY

For any work of architecture to be beautiful, all its elements must be correctly situated and be of the proper size, shape and colour.

Detail of the interior of the Nativity façade.

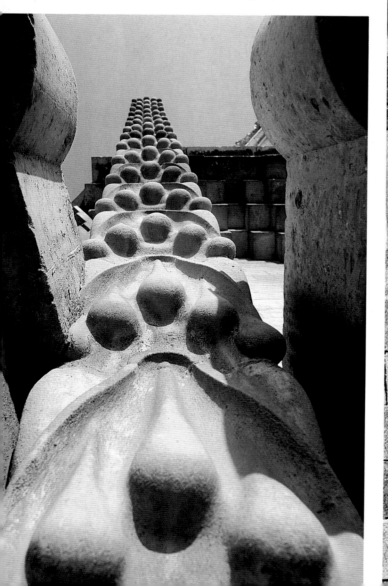

Alpha and Omaege, wheat tassles. Needles of the apse.

*Terminations
of the
belltowers.
Geometrical
composition
of the bodies
forming
intersections.*

a) *Nature.*

Gaudinian plasticity is based on the study of nature and is expressed in shapes and colours.

We have already seen that Gaudí spoke of what he had learned from nature: ''This tree, next to my workshop, is my master.'' From its observation he drew conclusions he then applied to his projects. The use of natural forms of flora and fauna is common throughout his work and in many of the details of the temple. Abstract geometrical forms are derived from the study of nature, resulting in the combination of blends and new forms never before used in architecture.

Local land and sea fauna magnificently decorate the apse.

A snail.   *A lizard.*

*Flight to Egypt
group.*

*Turtle that serves as
a base of a column
of the Nativity portal.*

*To suggest cold at Christmas, large icicles surround
the three Nativity portals.*

Corkscrew staircase. Spiral of skirting and concentric steps recall natural forms.

Porticoed gallery of Nativity façade interior.

b) *The form.*

Natural forms are already present in the capitals of the crypt and in the gargoyles and pinnacles of the apse. On the Nativity façade, the human figure, animals and plants are present expressing the mystery of Christmas, together with everything surrounding the childhood of Jesus. They are also found on the windows on the sculptural motifs representing fruits from different seasons of the year.

Geometrical forms based on simple elements and drawings become more complex as the study and use of warped surfaces becomes more familiar. He first makes use of hyperboloids and helicoids, obtaining a cluster of innovations as theoretical as they are formal.

The columns, windows and vaults projected in the later years of his life are the exponent of extraordinary study and work. This also true of the belltowers, the domes and other details.

Starred forms.

Detail of
the tower
part of the
Rosary
portal.

Wrought
iron torch
staff.

Portable pulpit.

Detail of the candelabrum. Wrought iron.

Detail of fence.

Sculpted brackets of Nativity façade interior.

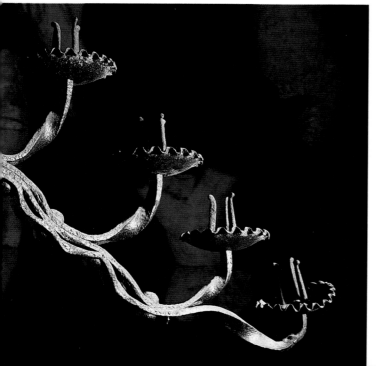

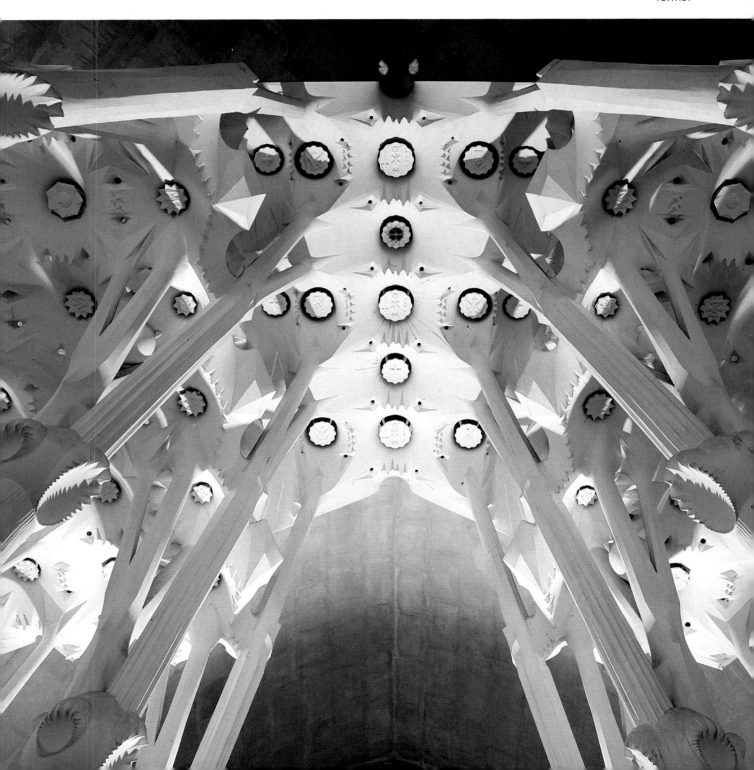

Vaults of nave, composition of ruled geometrical forms.

c) *Colour.*

Colour is also another important element in the architecture of Gaudí. In the temple, the tips of the belltowers are the remarkable result. A demonstration project can be seen in the 1/25 scale model of the Nativity façade which was presented in Paris in 1910; unfortunately, it was destroyed in 1936, though a part of Gaudinian theories have been applied based on it.

Model coloured by Jujol —1910—, restored.

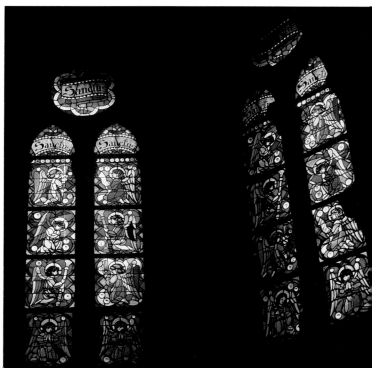

Belltowers terminations, colossal elements (25 m) of light and colour.

Soundwings studied to project musical sounds emitted by tubular bells.

to an improved visibility of the decorated surfaces. Spotlights placed at the mouths of the hyperboloids of the vaults add a softened light to the night that the stained glass windows, following the new procedure experimented in the cathedral of Mallorca, accompany with the maximum brilliance of the polychrome glass, with no paint or enamelwork. ''The temple will be very bright, with beautiful mixtures of light combining that coming from the high domes with that from the stained glass windows. All this will illuminate the polychrome interior,'' Gaudí explained.

Hollow of belltower terminations for placing reflectors.

d) Acoustics and lighting.

Gaudí had studied acoustical problems and had experimented with the tubular bells he placed in the long, hollow belltowers, in addition to the organs which would fill the naves with musical sounds.

A choir bay encircles the nave along the sides and interior of the back of the Glory façade, with a capacity for 1,500 singers. Above the ambulatory of the apse, he planned a children's choir for 700 voices. He placed the priests around the altar. He foresaw the participation of the people in the celebrations and, as with many other liturgical decisions, he was ahead of the II Vatican Council.

Light, harmoniously entering through the large windows and attenuated by the new geometrical surfaces, will avoid excessive contrast and contribute

From belltowers, bell chimes and light from reflectors aimed at the people.

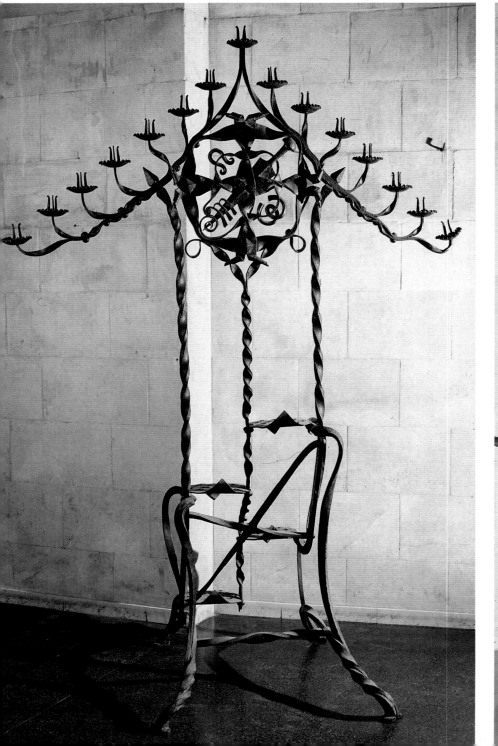

Candelabrum for Holy Week ceremonies.

Cross with candelabrum.

Apse stained-glass windows.

e) *Liturgical objects*

Gaudí projected, for worship in the temple crypt, the altars, objects and furniture, liturgically instructing us with the dignity and quality of each one: the benches, the sacristy cabinets, the pulpit and the confessionals, the candelabra and sideboards, the chairs for the officiants, the lamps and the chandeliers. The candlestand and the lectern are especially notable. He personally had a hand in making some of the pieces.

Paschal candle. Group.

Detail with open arms to be carried in procession.

Isidre Puig i Boada and Lluis Bonet i Garí, chief architects of the works, with their successor Jordi Bonet and the president of the Foundation of the Temple of the Sagrada Familia, Joan Antoni Maragall.

Francesc Berenguer and Llorenç Matamala, two loyal collaborators of the Master. Drawing by Opisso.

Belltower terminations of the Passion façade, constructed by the successors of Gaudí.

IV. 1. GAUDI'S SUCCESSORS

A fine group of architects, sculptors and other talented collaborators worked beside the Master. Until 1915, Francesc Berenguer — who Gaudí called his right hand — Joan Rubió, Josep M. Jujol, J. Canaleta, J.F. Ràfols, Domènec Sugrañes i F. Quintana. There were also Joan Matamala, Carles Mani and Opisso.

At Gaudí's death, Domènec Sugrañes continued as directing architect, assisted by F. Quintana. In the next ten years, the other three belltowers and the pinnacles that crown each portal were finished. Gaudí had said: ''I know the personal tastes of the architects that succeed me will have an influence on the work, and this does not bother me, but rather leads me to think that it will benefit the temple. It will mark the variance of time within the unity of the general plan.'' ''Great temples have never been the work of one single architect.''

Work was interrupted and Gaudí's workshop was destroyed by the revolution of 1936. The crypt was reconstructed in 1940 under the direction of F. Quintana, Sugrañes having died in 1938.

In 1954, the Board commited itself to build the Passion façade. The architects Isidre Puig i Boada and Lluís Bonet i Garí ''named members of the Building Board,'' collaborated with Quintana to direct the job, and succeeded him after his death in 1966. The sculptor Jaume Busquets made the Nativity group in 1959, and the Annunciation in 1967. F. Cardoner and F. Dapena collaborated on the work as assistant architects, and César Martinell and Joan Bergós contributed calculations and advice.

In 1977 the four pinnacles of the Passion façade were crowned. Gaudí had been dead for 50 years. As of 1982, Francesc Cardoner was named directing architect, and in 1985 Dr. in Architecture Jordi Bonet i Armengol was named director-coordinator for the whole project. The team was completed and expanded with the intervention of the sculptor Josep M. Subirachs and of architects Joan Margarit, Carles Buxadé; a new generation who had never met the Master.

Josep M. Subirachs diligently works on the Passion sculptures.

2. CURRENT STATE AND IMMEDIATE FUTURE

Today, only half of the building can be considered complete. The finished elements include the crypt, in the apse and Passion and Nativity façades and aisles; the walls of the crossing apse and the aisles and some sections of the cloister; the Passion and Nativity façades (though the pediment and many of the sculptures have still to be added to the latter); and the foundations of all the columns halfway to the transept. The columns supporting the singers' gallery and those of the nave and the transept of the Passion are complete and support the side vaults over an area of 1,000 m².

The faithful and friends of the temple of the Sagrada Familia are the support that spiritually makes the idea move forward, and the works continue with contributions of all sorts — large and small — collected everyday. Added to this is the selfless dedication of all those who work at the site: technicians, masons, sculptors and stone-cutters, mechanics, carpenters, etc.

Administration is austere, which is how the work being done is accommodated to income coming in from all sorts of donations. The temple is expiatory and therefore can be built only with donations.

Technically, the most modern technology is used and computers are employed to calculate the structure or work the stone, together with the quality-control of the stone and concrete and the machinery for shoring up the foundation.

People ask themselves: When will it be finished? This is difficult to say because it is conditioned by the donations received, but there is a programme for the present and one for the coming future which accomplishes the proposals of the Foundation Board.

Stone-cutters' workshop.

Present state of the works of the nave.

Cranes lift pre-fabricated window pieces.

It took Gaudí 40 to 50 years to raise one façade and the walls of the apse. The upheaval caused by the Spanish Civil War left the work at a standstill for around 20 years. The generation of those who knew him –his direct followers– took 20 years to build the Passion façade. The nave and aisles should now be covered by the end of the century. If this can be done, the other vaults could be completed by the early-21st century. But there is still much to be done before the dome can be built and the roofs completed, along with the Glory façade and, in short, all Gaudí planned for his masterpiece.

Stone-cutters sculpt Montjuic stone by hand.

IV. 3. THE LOVERS OF THE TEMPLE

"The temple of Sagrada Familia is built by the people and mirrors their way of being;" "At the Sagrada Familia everything is providential," Gaudí often said, and added: "This will be the temple of the Catalonia of today. I remember once being told that Catalonia had never been anything historically, and I answered that if this were true it would be one more reason to believe that it was still meant to be something and for that we must work."

It was the poet Joan Maragall, a good friend of Gaudí, who first grasped the transcendence of the work of the Master and was its first promoter in the press. His enthusiastic articles made extensively known that which was hard to understand, even though the simple people had already reacted favourably to the proposal and the trust which

President Prat de la Riba and Bishop Reig listen to explanations of Gaudí.

together with the Association de Followers of St. Joseph, J.M. Bocabella and M. Dalmases had expressed to him and Torras i Bages had praised.

But the articles "The Temple That Grows" (1900), "A Grace of Charity," etc., despite their clear and forceful stand, do not have the prophetic force of the verses of "New Ode to Barcelona," especially since it was written after the Setmana Tràgica or Tragic Week, (July 1909), which was a sad expression of the problems that the Catalan social forces faced. Joan Maragall, as a poet, prophetically sees the temple Gaudí dreamt of, in spite of the hate and flames which, a few years later would attempt to rub out and destroy the symbols of identity of the Catalan people:

Joan Maragall (drawing by R. Casas) enthusiastic propagator of the Sagrada Familia.

To the east, mystic example,
like a giant flower blossoms a temple
amazed at having been born here
amidst a people so sullen and nasty
who laugh and swear and fight and huff
against all that is human and divine.
But, amidst misery and rage and smoke,
the temple (who cares!) rises and prospers
awaiting a faithful yet to come.

Papal nuncio Mons. Rangonesi, listening to Gaudí, exclaimed, ''You are the Dante of architecture.''

Torras i Bages and Gaudí, drawing by Opisso.

El Reverent sacerdot Torras i Bages i l'arquitecte "Anton" Gaudí

Japanese architect Kenji I may visited the temple in 1926 and became a propagator of Gaudí in Japan.

Visit of the princes of Japan, Aki Hito and Michiko, to the temple of the Sagrada Familia.

Many circumstances attempted to eliminate the temple. The schools were destroyed. All of Gaudí's studio disappeared, but not his spirit. Gradually, everyone went back to work and the four belltowers of the Passion façade were raised.

Interest in Gaudí reawakened with the centennial of his birth (1952). Until then, no art history textbook, no famous writer had heard of him. Ten years after his death, only a few faithful disciples had published books extolling his figure or even mentioned him. With the controversy surrounding the continuation or not of the works of the temple, once again the arguments that began with the silence surrounding the last years of the Master's life emerge.

But the people remain faithful. ''The temple of the Sagrada Familia is expiatory. This means it must be nourished with sacrifices; if it were unable to nourish itself, it would be a blasphemous work and would never be finished.'' ''The word expiatory is what revolts sectarians.''

And bequests and donations arrive. The collection, announced one Sunday a year, collects more and more donations. ''It is a work in the hands of God and in the will of the people,'' Gaudí repeated.

And Catalans have responded generously, have fallen in love with the temple that grows, their Temple. And as Gaudí would prophetically say: ''People from all over the world will come to admire it.'' Its image has

A group of visitors admire the sculptures of the Passion façade.

Autograph of the secretary general of the United Nations, Javier Pérez de Cuéllar.

Celebration of Palm Sunday, seen from the Passion façade.

become part of the city of Barcelona.

A few months after the death of Gaudí, a young Japanese architect, Kenji Imai, came to Barcelona. He wanted to meet Gaudí, just as he had done in the United States with Frank Lloyd Wright, in Germany with Walter Gropius and in Paris with Le Corbusier. He was unable to meet the Master, but was so impressed with his work that he made it known in his country. He even dared construct the cathedral of Nagasaki, following the ideas that the study of Gaudí's work had inspired in him. The Japanese

Homenaje a un artista
universal, gloria del genio catalán.

22 de Mayo de 1986

John Paul II visited the temple of the Sagrada Familia on November 7, 1982.

visited by all the great personalities of politics, the arts and the sciences. A temple under construction, an oddity, an expression of solidarity, faith and hope, it is love, the brotherhood of all men. Christians believe that, through Jesus Christ, we are all brothers, that love is the source of life and that we will resurrect in a new life. That is why the temple of the Sagrada Familia is a holy place open to all to gather together as children of one God, to praise, to sing and to pray. To offer glory to God, the Catalans are raising this work, unique in the world, with the determination of a faithful who still come and who desire the monumental idea of Gaudí to be carried to an end.

As lovers of this legacy, people of various places and colours work in its construction, and all who have heard speak about it and wish to share in a solidarity that extends all over the earth, come to visit and contribute.

Relief by Josep Llimona showing main altar of crypt.

come to visit the works of Gaudí, and they realize he is one of the great masters of modern architecture.

In the 50s, Gropius visited the chapel of the Güell Colony. For more than an hour he remained in silent contemplation of that marvel. Le Corbusier, on his first visit to Barcelona in 1927, reproduced the temple schools in his sketches and later wrote of Gaudí: "He is the great builder of this century."

In 1961, in Paris, at the exhibit "The Origins of the Twentieth Century," the worth of Gaudí which had not been valued in 1910, was finally recognized.

In Italy, England, Holland, Germany or New Zealand (the other side of the world), as elsewhere in the world, the originality of Gaudí is considered one of the highest exponents of art of all times.

The Holy Father, John Paul II, on his visit to Barcelona, went through the Sagrada Familia. It is

Antoni Gaudí, on day of Corpus Christi celebration in 1924, attending procession on the steps of cathedral of Barcelona.

WORLD		CATALONIA AND SPAIN		GAUDI. TEMPLE OF THE SAGRADA FAMILIA	
		1833	Oda *La Pàtria* (B.C. Aribau)		
		1835	Convents burned		
			(B) Felip Pedrell		
1840	(B) Auguste Rodin				
		1841	Publication of *Lo gaiter del Llobregat* (Rubió i Ors)		
			(B) Valentí Almirall		
		1842	Restoration of University of Barcelona		
		1845	(B) Jacint Verdaguer (poeta)		
1846	Coronation of Pius IX	1846	(B) Josep Torras i Bages		
1848	II French Republic	1848	(D) Jaume Balmes		
		1850	(B) Lluís Domènech i Montaner		
			Foundation Catalan Fine Arts Academy of St. George		
				1852	(B, VI/25) Antoni Gaudí
1853	Japan opens trade with West				
		1859	Restoration of Floral Games		
1863	(B) Aristides Maillol	1860	(B) Joan Maragall		
1863/65	American Civil War	1861	(B) Santiago Rusiñol		
1864	I International	1863	Foundation Association Followers St. Joseph	1863/69	Studies at the Escolapios of Reus
		1867	(B) Lluís Millet		
			(B) Josep Puig i Cadafalch		
1868	(B) Gandhi	1868	September Revolution		
			(B) Francesc Vidal i Barraquer		
			(B) Enric Prat de la Riba		
1870	(B) Lenin	1870	(D) Sant Antoni M. Claret		
	(D) Charles Dickens		(D) Joan Prim, assassinated		
	Franco-Prussian War				
	End of Papal States				
1871	First perfomance of *Aïda*, by Verdi			1871	Enters university
	Proclamation of II German Reich				
		1873	I Republic		
1874	Birth of Impressionism, in Paris	1874	(D) Marià Fortuny		
		1875	Restoration of Alfonso XII	1875/78	Gaudí works with Villar and Fontserè
		1876	Foundation Centre Excursionista Catalonia		
			(B) Pau Casals.		
		1877	Publication *L'Atlàntida* (J. Verdaguer)		
1878	(D) Pius IX			1878	Architect degree
1879	(B) Albert Einstein				
				1880	Casa Vicens
1881	First perfomance of *Parsifal*, by Richard Wagner	1881	Proclamation Our Lady of Montserrat, Patron of Catalonia		
			(B) P.R. Picasso		
1882	(B) I. Stravinsky			1882	(III/19) Corner-stone of Temple of Sagrada Família
1883	(B) W. Gropius			1883	(XI/3) A. Gaudí Architect of T. of Sagrada Família
	(D) Richard Wagner				
		1884	Modernism		
			(B) Josep Carner		
			(D) M. Milà i Fontanals		
		1885	Publication *Canigó* (J. Verdaguer)	1885	Blessing of chapel of St. Joseph (T. Sagrada Família)
				1885/90	Güell Palace
		1886	Publication *Lo Catalanisme* (V. Almirall)		
1887	(B) Le Corbusier				
		1888	I Universal Exposition of Barcelona	1888/96	Astorga
1889	II International				
				1889/92	Teresian School
				1890	Drawing complete Temple, 1st solution
		1891	Foundation «Orfeó Català»		
		1892	Bases de Manresa	1892	Bequest of 800,000 ptas.
			La tradició catalana (Torras i Bages)		Nativity façade begun
		1893	Foundation of Artistic Circle of St. Luke		
			Restoration of Ripoll		
			Bomb at the Liceu		
1895	Invention of cinema (Lumière brothers)				
1896	(D) Alfred Nobel			1896	Naming of 1st Board by Bishop Català
	(D) César Franck				
		1898	Spanish-American War	1898/1902	Casa Calvet
			Loss of Cuba, Puerto Rico and Philippines	1898/1914	Güell Colony
		1899	Torras i Bages, Bishop of Vic		
		1900	*El temple que neix* (Maragall)	1900	Cloister of the Rosary
1901	(D) Verdi	1901	Foundation of Lliga Regionalista	1901/1915	Parc Güell
	Invention of radio, Marconi				
		1902	(D) Jacint Verdaguer		
			Coronation of Alfonso XIII		
1903	(D) Leo XIII	1903	Foundation of F.A.D.	1903/08	Casa Batlló
				1903/15	Cathedral of Mallorca
				1903/11	Casa Milà
				1904	Alfonso XIII visits Temple
1905	Russo-Japanese War			1905	Article by Maragall: *A Grace of Charity*
	Theory of relativity				
1906	(D) P. Cézanne	1906	*La Nacionalitat Catalana* (Prat de la Riba)		
			I Int. Congress of the Catalan Language		
			"Noucentisme"		
		1907	Solidaritat Catalana		
			Foundation of the «Institut d'Estudis Catalans»		
		1909	Tragic Week	1909	Parish schools of the Sagrada Família
			Oda nova a Barcelona (Maragall)		
				1910	Gaudí Exhibit, in Paris
		1911	(D) Isidre Nonell	1911	Gaudí suffers Malta fever, Puigcerdà
			(D) Joan Maragall		
1912	(D) Pius X			1912	Sixty-metre belltowers
	Republic of China				
1914	World War I	1914	Mancomunitat of Catalonia (IV/6)		
	Manufacture of Ford Model T				
		1915	Liturgical Congress of Montserrat		
		1916	(D) Torras i Bages (II/7)	1916	Visit by Papal nuncio Rangonessi
					Gaudí asks for donations from people of Barcelona
1917	(D) A. Rodin	1917	(D) Prat de la Riba (VIII/3)	1917/18	Publication drawing of Passion Façade
	Russian Revolution				
1918	End of World War I				

WORLD	CATALONIA AND SPAIN	GAUDÍ. TEMPLE DE LA SAGRADA FAMÍLIA
1919 Foundation of Bauhaus / Versailles Treaty		1919/20 Model of sacristy, on 1/25 scale
		1921 Final study of belltower needles
1922 (D) Benedict XV	1923 Dictatorship of Primo de Rivera / (D) Lluís Domènech i Montaner / (D) Àngel Guimerà	1923 Model of Temple interior, on 1/10 scale
1923 *Vers une architecture* (Le Corbusier)		
	1925 Josep Clarà, Grand Prize (Paris)	1924 Arrest of Gaudí (September 11)
		1925 Belltower of St. Barnabas finished (XI/30)
		1926 (D) Death of Gaudí (VI/10)
	1928 Yellow Manifesto	1928 *Gaudí* (Ràfols-Folguera)
1929 Lateran Pacts	1929 II International Exhibition Barcelona	1929 *El Temple Sagrada Família* (I. Puig i Boada)
	1930 Creation of GATCPAC	1930 Belltowers of Nativity façade finished
	1931 Proclamation of the Republic / Millenium of Montserrat	
	1932 Statute of Catalonia / Fabra dictionary	
1933 F. D. Roosevelt elected president of U.S.A. / End of Bauhaus / III German Reich	1933 Macià Plan	
1934 Charter of Athens		
1935 *La ville radieuse* (Le Corbusier)		
	1936 Military uprising / Revolution / Spanish Civil War	1936 Special edition of ''El Matí'', dedicated to Gaudí / Destruction of Gaudí's study / Temple of Sagrada Família is burned
1937 Sino-Japanese War		
		1938 (D) Architect Sugrañes
1939 World War II / (D) Pius XI	1939 End of Spanish Civil War	
1940 W. Churchill prime minister of U.K.	1940 (D) Lluís Companys, President of the Generalitat, executed	1940 Restoration of the crypt
1941 Japan attacks Pearl Harbor		
	1943 (D) Cardenal Vidal i Barraquer, in exile	
1945 Germanay surrenders / End of World War II / U.N. constituted, San Francisco	1945 J. M. Sert, paintings in Cathedral of Vic	
1946 Foundation of UNESCO / Council of Europe constituted		
	1947 Celebrations enthronement Our Lady of Montserrat	
1949 Victory of Mao Ze Dong, in China	1950 Madona of Portlligat, Salvador Dalí	
1950 Korean War	1952 Int. Eucharistic Congress in Barcelona	1952 Gaudí Centennial Exhibit, Barcelona
	1953/68 J.L. Sert, dean of Harvard School of Architecture	1954 Passion façade begun
		1956 Barcelona column, 1st collection
	1957 (D) J. Puig i Cadafalch	1958 Pius XII exhorts construction
		1961 Gaudí Exhibition in Paris, in ''Les Sources XXème siècle»
1962/68 II Vatican Council	1963 Declarations of Abbot Escarré to ''Le Monde»	
1963 (D) John XXIII / (D) President J. F. Kennedy, assassinated		1964 Gaudía Exhibit in Madrid
		1965 Paul VI blesses the work
		1967 (D) Architect Quintana / I. Puig i Boada, Architect Director
1969 Man lands on the Moon (VII/21	1969 ''Trade'' building (J.A. Coderch) / Narcís Jubany, Archbishop of Barcelona	
1971 (D) I. Stravinsky	1971 ''Assemblea de Catalunya''	1971 Lluís Bonet i Garí, Architect Director
	1972 ''Miró Foundation'' (J.L. Sert)	
	1973 (D) Pau Casals	
	1975 (D) General Franco / Juan Carlos I, King of Spain	
	1977 Return of President Tarradellas	1977 Four Passion belltowers finished
1978 (D) Paul VI / Election of John Paul II	1979 Statute of Catalonia	
	1980 Jordi Pujol, President of the Generalitat	1982 John Paul Ii visits the Temple
		1985 Jordi Bonet i Armengol, Architect Coordinator and Director
	1986 Barcelona, chosen to host the 1992 Olympic Games	
	1988/89 Millenium of Catalonia	1988 Calculations of nave foundation (architects Margarit and Buxadé) / J. M. Subirachs begins sculptures
1989 Coronation of Emperor Aki Hito of Japan / Berlin Wall comes down		1989 Gaudí exhibit in Japan
	1990 III Liturgical Congress of Montserrat	1990 Final foundations of nave / The columns are raised
1991 URSS end	1990 III Liturgical Congress of Montserrat / Ricard M. Carles Archbishop of Barcelona	1990 Nave foundations completed / Columns erected
1991 Collapse of the Soviet Union		1991 Agreement with UPC to draw the vaults in the nave and aisles
1992 Gulf War / German Unification / Clinton elected US President	1992 Barcelona Olympic Games / Expo in Seville	1992 First section of the singers' gallery
1993 War in the ex-Yugoslavia / Maastricht Treaty		1993 Deaths of Lluis Bonet Garí and J. A. Maragall
1995 Peace in Bosnia		1995 First section of 30 metre-high aisle vaults
1996 Olympic Games in Atlanta, USA	1996 PP takes over from PSOE in government / IUA Congress in Barcelona / Death of Cardinal Narcís Jubany	1996 Side vaults closed (1,000 m²)
		1997 First section of nave

V. 2. THE VISIT

Today, starting from the entrance in Plaça de la Sagrada Família, one can visit:

– The Façade of the Passion, work on which continues. A lift takes visitors to a height of 90 metres.

– The interior of what will be the cathedral, between the eight points of the east and west front belltowers.

– The apse and its walls with their long windows, the crossing columns and the nave.

– The aisles and their vaults and singers' galleries, along with part of the vaults in the nave.

– The whole of the Nativity Façade, where a lift takes visitors up to a height of 60 metres.

– The monographic museum, showing the history of the church and many of Antoni Gaudí's original plaster models, liturgical objects, photos, plans, etc. A special exhibition room contains some twenty original drawings by Gaudí.

In the crypt, open for the services of the parish church, are the tombs of Gaudí and the founders of the building.

The map shows the location of the main elements, giving information which can be complemented at the administrative offices of the Temple Expiatori de la Sagrada Família.

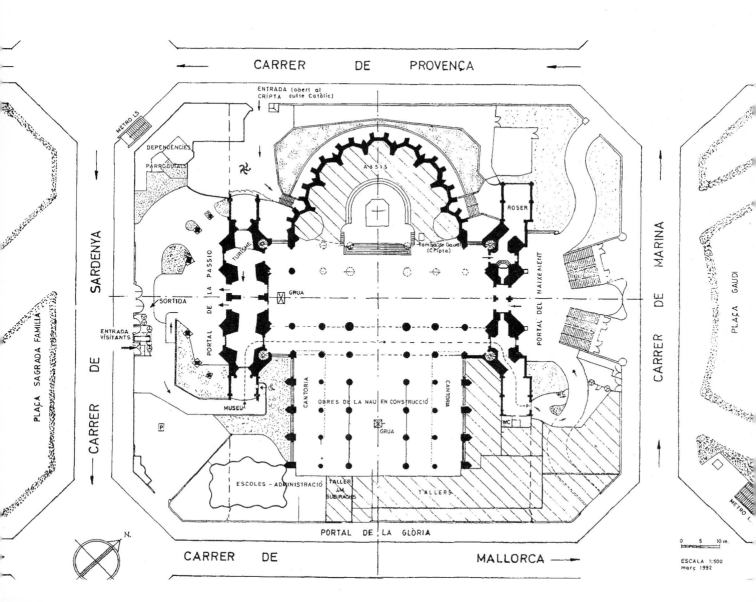

V. 3. BIBLIOGRAPHY

Bassegoda Nonell, J.: «GAUDÍ», Ed. Salvat, 1985.
—«EL GRAN GAUDÍ», Ed. Ausa, 1989.
Bassegoda Nonell, J., i Collins, G.: «PORTAFOLIO».
Bergós, J.: «GAUDÍ, L'HOME I L'OBRA», Ed. Ariel, 1954.
Maragall, J.: «EL TEMPLE DE LA SAGRADA FAMÍLIA». Recull d'articles. 1986.
Martinell, C.: «GAUDÍ, SU VIDA, SU TEORÍA, SU OBRA», Col.legi Oficial d'Arquitectes de Catalunya i Balears, 1967.
—«GAUDÍ I LA SAGRADA FAMÍLIA».
Moya, Ll.: «EL TEMPLE DE LA SAGRADA FAMÍLIA, 1882-1982», Ed. JTSF, 1982.
Puig Boada, I.: «EL TEMPLE DE LA SAGRADA FAMÍLIA», Ed. Barcino, 1929.
—«EL TEMPLE DE LA SAGRADA FAMÍLIA», Ed. Thor, 1979.
—«EL PENSAMENT DE GAUDÍ», Col.legi Oficial d'Arquitectes de Catalunya, 1981.
Ràfols, J. F.: «GAUDÍ», Ed. Canosa, 1928.
Tarragó, J.: «GAUDÍ», Ed. Escudo de Oro, 1974.

Table of contents